Streams of text have been written since the Musée d'Orsay opened out, as this special issue of «Beaux-Arts» shows, a museum is above all works of art and walls to show them on. Just about everything there is to say has been said about the selection of works and the somewhat controversial museography. But a museum is also a public, the people who come to look, learn and admire art. Since December 1986, when the «M'O» opened its doors, some 10 million people have done just this.

With the help of hindsight, it is now possible to draw up a preliminary balance-sheet. We curators know where the museum's weakeness lie (insufficient space in certain areas and unsatisfactory lighting in a few others), and will be able to gradually correct them. But one thing is certain: the major challenge of the museum has been met: to interest the public in the heritage of the 19th century.

The museum collections have been considerably enriched. Among the new works the painting department has acquired are canvases by Daubigny, Bonnard, Van Gogh and Redon. Other additions are objets d'art (from Kolo Moser to Lalique), sculpture (from Doré to Camille Claudel), and photographs and drawings (from Nadar to Baudelaire, and from Degas to Seurat). The finest of these works, displayed for the public to admire in 1990, sum up seven years of acquisitions. They go to prove that the M'O is not only a mere storehouse of the past but a living museum.

Françoise Cachin
Directress, Musée d'Orsay

TABLE OF CONTENTS

Directeur de la publication : Jean-Noël Beyler. Rédacteur en chef : Jérôme Coignard. Responsable du développement : Christophe Lagrange. Coordination : Laurence Madeline. Directeur artistique : Ruedi Baur. Maquette : Gilles Vincent. Traduction : Lois Grjebine. Secrétariat de rédaction : Pascal Steichen. Légendes des illustrations : Philippe Dufour, Thalie Goetz, Caroline Larroche, Laurence Madeline. Publié par Beaux-Arts Magazine, Publications Nuit et Jour, 9, rue Christiani, 75018 Paris. Tél. : 49.25.17.17. Télex : 281 544F. Télécopie : 49.25.17.21. RCS Nanterre 326 216 389 0014. Commission paritaire 65094. Photocomposition : Cicero. Imprimé en Italie. Nous remercions, pour l'aide qu'ils nous ont apportée à la réalisation de ce volume, Françoise Cachin, directeur du musée d'Orsay, Aggy Lerolle, chef du service de presse, Geneviève Lacambre, Anne Pingeot, conservateurs en chef, Marc Bascou, Chantal Georgel, Françoise Heilbrun, Caroline Mathieu, Philippe Néagu, Jean-Michel Nectoux, conservateurs, Nicole Savy, chargée de la littérature au musée d'Orsay, Odile Billoret, directrice de la librairie d'Orsay, Béatrice de Boisséson, chef du service photographique de la Réunion des musées nationaux, Frédérique Kartouby.
Crédits photographiques : © RMN sauf mention contraire.
Jacques-Emile Blanche, Pierre Bonnard, Emile Bernard, Joseph Bernard, Giovanni Boldini, Rupert Carabin, Camille Claudel, Maurice Denis, Hans Jorgen Diehl, Henri Gervex, René Lalique, Aristide Maillol, Claude Monet, Pierre-Auguste Renoir, Auguste Rodin, Edouard Vuillard, Félix Vallotton, Paul Sérusier, © by Spadem.
Antoine Bourdelle, Théo van Rysselberghe, © by Adagp.
Henri Matisse, © Succession H. Matisse.

PAINTING

The collections that are now together at the Musée d'Orsay originally came from the Louvre, the Jeu de Paume, the Musée National d'Art Moderne, as well as the Musée du Luxembourg, which was established as early as 1818 to show the works of living artists. These collections are for the most part the result of selections of contemporary pieces made during the 19th century, as well as reactions to these choices. Many works were acquired during the successive Salons, which were reserved almost exclusively for French painters till 1890, at which time the doors were opened to foreign artists. Large donations at the turn of the century made these collections better balanced: Millet's "Angélus", for example, was donated by Chauchard and Manet's "Le Déjeuner sur l'Herbe" by Moreau-Nélaton. It was also thanks to such donations that a museum devoted to the Impressionists at the Jeu de Paume was opened to the public in 1947 and became so popular that it proved too small to accomodate the crowds. Meanwhile, the once famous works at the Musée du Luxembourg went into museum reserves for a full half-century. It was therefore high time that the paintings of the period be presented to the public in their rich diversity, using no other criteria than their quality as works of art. The presentation at the Musée d'Orsay respects the affiliations that the artists themselves established and is in chronological order: the preeminence of the Salon during the Second Empire, the disruptive effect of the independent exhibitions starting with the Impressionnists, and the internationalization of art at the turn of the century. The last room in the museum shows recent acquisitions.

Geneviève Lacambre, Chief Curator.

Winslow Hower,
Summer's Night,
1890, oil on canvas.

James MacNeil
Whistler,
*Arrangement in Grey
and Black, Portrait of
the Artist's Mother,*
1871, oil on canvas.

Henri Gervex, *Une
Séance de Jury de
Peinture*, 1885, oil on
canvas.

LITERATURE

Literature has a place in the Musée d'Orsay, first and foremost with the portraits of such world-famous poets and writers as Charles Baudelaire, Emile Zola, Stéphane Mallarmé or Marcel Proust by Courbet (in a corner of his "L'Atelier"), by Manet or by Jacques-Emile Blanche. These 75 years of history are also presented in dossier-exhibitions, like the ones devoted to journalism, Bohemian life, or "The Century of Dictionaries", which constituted diverse approaches to the literary movements of the period. Literature is also given a place in the lectures, panel discussions and courses devoted to history and to art history that are held in the museum, and which are published in "48/14". Indeed, during the 1848-1914 period, the bonds between text and image were sometimes especially strong, as artists and writers defended common concerns in their drive to give birth to what is now called "modern" art.
Nicole Savy, Head of Literature Section.

Jacques-Emile Blanche, *Portrait de Marcel Proust*, oil on canvas.

INTRODUCTION

Since the Musée d'Orsay opened in December 1986, the public has flocked to see its collections and its reputation has grown so rapidly that it now ranks among the world's great museums. What explains its phenomenal success? Right from the start, the museum had a number of trump cards. But it also had some poor ones: to begin with, the building itself, an abandoned railroad station. People have become so accustomed to the idea of turned a station into an art centre that it seems quite simple. But the problem was not quite that straightforward. Not only were there serious technical problems, but the way in which the gigantic interior space could be put to use posed other major problems. The solution was left to the ACT team that won the international competition in 1979 and to Gae Aulenti who the following year was put in charge of the interior design and the museography. In fact, the architects were not to touch the outside of the building, designed by Laloux in 1900.

What happened next was something of a miracle. Till the museum project came along, the building had attracted little attention, so little that some people were quite prepared to let it to be torn down. It was paradoxically the creation of the museum that made people perceive the architectural quality of the building. All you have to do is cross the Pont Royal bridge to understand that the building was originally designed, with a certain gracefulness, as the pendant on the Left Bank of the Flore wing of the Louvre, just as its contents today are a direct continuation of the collections on the other side of the river.

The renaissance of the old train station is most likely due not only to its architectural qualities but also to what could be called the Parisians' complex about what was done to Les Halles. Unlike the famous Baltard pavilions that were torn down at Les Halles to make way for the present Forum, the train station was saved in part because of the rediscovery of 19th-century art starting in the 1960s.

But this rediscovery, which is the reason why the project was initiated, could just as easily have constituted a second drawback. Once the building was

SCULPTURE

The abundance of sculpture created during the 19th century was matched only by the extent of its destruction from World War I through the 1970s. Four great names stand out to remind us of a prolific half-century of creation: Carpeaux, Rodin, Bourdelle and Maillol. Hundreds more were lost to history. The rediscovery of 19th-century French sculpture began outside the country, and only then did the trend catch on in France. A major exhibition, ''French Sculpture of the 19th Century'', held at the Grand-Palais in 1986, marked a high point in this rediscovery. The opening of the Musée d'Osrsay constitutes a landmark which we trust will be permanent. The first thing that greets the visitor's eye beneath the immense vault of the museum is an array of sculpture. (It was precisely because the glass vaulting let in so much light that sculpture was given pride of place!) The roster of artists shown gives a good idea of the various trends in 19th-century sculpture: David, Rude, Barye, Pradier, Clésinger, Carpeaux, Daumier, Frémiet, Degas, Gauguin, Lacombe, Rodin, Camille Claudel, Dalou, Maillol and Bourdelle. Their works are reminders that sculpture is essentially a monumental art that serves memory and the powers that be (civilian and religious) by its quality, its permanence and consequently by its usefulness as propaganda. Today this sculpture, which appeals to the knowledgeable art-lover as well as to the general public.

Anne Pingeot, Chief Curator.

View of the mainhall and the centeraisle.

Edgar Degas, *Petite Danseuse de Quatorze Ans* or *Grande Danseuse Habillée*, bronze, tulle ballet skirt, pink satin ribbon.

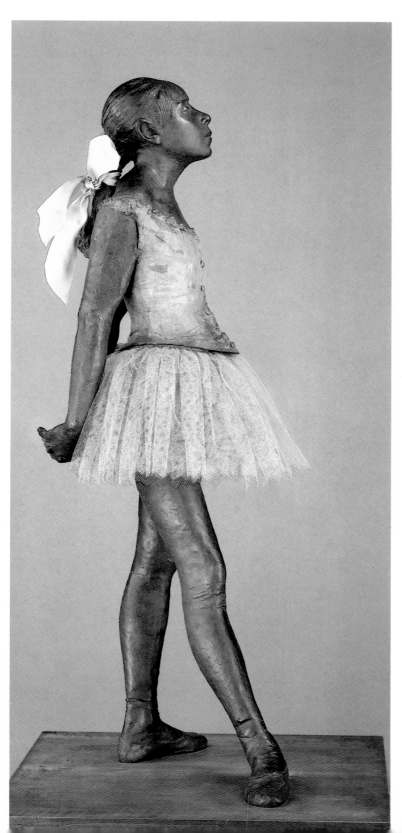

ARCHITECTURE

Was it conceivable that architecture be neglected when the Musée d'Orsay itself is housed in the striking iron and glass structure designed by Victor Lanoux? The Musée d'Orsay is in fact the first museum in France to treat architecture as a major art form, alongside painting and sculpture. Special sections have been set aside, such as the one for the Paris Opera and another for one of the large pavilions with a clock tower that was part of the old train station. In each are models, paintings, sculpture and drawings that evoke one of the biggest construction sites of the Second Empire, the extraordinary urban growth that took place during the life and times of Napoleon III, the town planner Baron Haussmann and France's Third Republic.

A temporary exhibition devoted to the Chicago school of architecture was to be the first of a series that has treated such subjects as architecture as a career, the opening of the new Opera house, architect Victor Laloux, the Champs-Elysees Theatre and hospital architecture. The museum recently organized a major restrospective on the Eiffel tower and the 1889 Exposition Universelle.

The core of the collection of drawings came from the Louvre and includes works by the leading architects of the time: Labrouste, Baltard, Hittorff, Lefuel, Viollet-le-Duc, and Duban. To this were added a number of acquisitions, as well as entire collections comprised of projects as well as sketches, drawings, correspondence and the like that were generously donated by the descendents of Gustave Eiffel, Ruprich-Robert, Guilleminault, Varcollier and the art founder Monduit. Architects and sculptors often worked together on furniture and interior decoration, and a large number of sketches by Lalique, Majorelle and Moser, among others, was bought. Thanks to generous donors, the museum boasts a splendid set of 2,000 drawings by Gallé and several hundred by the sculptor Antoine Zoegger.
Caroline Mathieu,
Curator.

revamped, the future museum became a verbal battlefield. One camp was fighting for a complete rehabilitation of the 19th century, and thought there were not enough Cormons, Géromes and Cabanels. The other camp was afraid that good taste would forever be corrupted at the sight of the academic paintings that the other camp threatened to rehabilitate. Even some artists found it scandalous that the official art of the Third Republic was being shown once again.

In fact, the Musée d'Orsay had a temporizing effect: war never broke out, because the 19th-century "avant-garde" painters and academic painters were hung in separate rooms. Rather than a proper reconciliation, the two camps learned to live side by side. This was a wise decision, for even the best painting by Bastien-Lepage would have trouble living up to a Gauguin or a Seurat; the Impressionist collection that was formerly at the Jeu de Paume museum seems destined to remain a separate paradise within the confines of the Musée d'Orsay.

It would nonetheless be a mistake to think that the creation of the Musée d'Orsay has not affected our knowledge of the 19th century.

The year 1848 marks the starting point in time for works at the Musée d'Orsay. It served to determine by and large what would stay at the Louvre and what would be at the Musée d'Orsay. Though the works of Delacroix and Ingres, both of whom painted well beyond that time-marker, remained at the Louvre, those of Courbet, Millet, Corot and Rousseau were moved in part or in toto to the Musée d'Orsay because they provide excellent illustrations of changing tastes in the arts that occurred around 1848.

The year 1914 marks the outer time-limit of the Museum. It corresponds to the outbreak of World War I, but in the arts, the break is not so clearcut. That is why the avant-garde movements of ther early 20th century, life Fauvism in 1905, are now at the Pompidou Centre and not at Orsay.

In addition to works from the Louvre and the famous collection of Impressionist paintings formerly in the Jeu de Paume are the Neo-Impressionist canvases that

Longitudinal corss-section of the Opera House, executed by Atelier Rome, under the direction of Richard Peduzzi.

PHOTOGRAPHY

It was only natural that one of the outstanding inventions of the 19th century, photography, have a place at the Musée d'Orsay. In 1979 a collection was started from scratch that emphasized visual creation but which included documentary photos, so important in the 19th century, which are by no means two mutually exclusive propositions. Acquisitions account for a good part of the collection, though there were also some large donations and a few loans from other institutions. All in all, there are some 15,000 works, in the form of original prints or negatives on paper, that run from 1839 to 1918. From the aesthetic point of view, this period can

be considered as the breeding ground for modern photography. The richest part of the collection is, of course, French but given the international stature of the museum, much effort has been expended to acquire foreign works, among them English, American and Italian works that till recently had been poorly represented in French collections.

In the field of photography, the museum has multifarious goals: to protect the nation's photographic heritage; to fill certain gaps in the national collections by acquiring works by such great artists as the Nadar brothers, Lewis Carroll or J.M. Cameron, as well as to help the public discover the works of such

amateur photographers as Pierre Bonnard, Henri Rivière or Victor Hugo at his studio in Jersey; to further research on the history of photography, a field that is just beginning to be explored; and of course to help the public understand and come to love the art of photography. To these ends, the museum organizes more or less big and ambitious exhibitions, accompanied or not by publications. (Old photographs, though fragile, are shown on a rotating basis.) Since the collection was begun two years ago, the Museum's policy has borne fruit; an interested public now exists, whereas only a few short years ago photography was largely ignored or looked down upon.
Françoise Heilbrun and Philippe Néagu, Curators.

Pierre Bonnard, *Modèle dans l'Atelier de l'Artiste*, around 1912, silver image.

Charles Aubry, *Anemones*, 1864-1865, print on albumenized paper from a glass negative with collodion, in the Mobilier National reserves.

Clarence Hudson White, *The Kiss*, 1904, platinum print.

HISTORY

The Musée d'Orsay decided in 1981 to extend its activities to such new areas as history, the illustrated press and illustrated books, and especially the cinema. The primary goal was to present a visual history of the period during which the works of art shown in the museum were created. With this in mind, a large circular showcase called an "Opening onto History" was set up using a number of symbolic objects, as well as pictures and texts, to outline the history of France from 1848 to 1914. Visitors can put their questions to a set of adjacent interactive "date machines", which give them access to over 600 historical events, 150 biographies and 150 subjects of historical interest. The guiding principle was to establish connections between the different kinds of facts that are stored in separate compartments of our memories, as they are in the museum, whereas a true understanding of any given civilisation requires that such facts be grasped in their entirety. Thus, by questioning these "memory machines", visitors are able to find out, say, what was happening at the time when Manet was painting his "Olympia" and put this artistic creation into context. Last but not least, the 19th century can be considered as a "century of images", for it was the time when images began to be reproduced in great quantities, put into movement and projected. That was why the museum felt it necessary to devote space to the 19th-century press, which opened up a whole new world of images to the public, and which deeply affected writers, musicians and artists alike. The same holds true for that other creation of the period, the cinema, which was to quickly carve out a place for itself as a major art form.
Chantal Georgel, Curator.

a few hundred people took the trouble to see at the Palais de Tokyo as of 1977 and some works that had been in other, smaller museums. Most of the latter had been at the Musée du Luxembourg, which had been turned into a Museum for Living Artists by Louis-Philippe and radically transformed in 1937 into a modern art museum. An energetic acquisition policy allowed the Musée d'Orsay to fill the gaps in its collection. There is no point in lamenting the fact that a large number of paintings by Monet and Gauguin, among others, have gone into permanent exile. Nor will it make things any better to deplore the fact that the collection of foreign works is so small. Still, now that canvases by Bocklin, Munch and Klimt have been added, Paris no longer seems to be quite so self-centred.

There are four areas — sculpture, objets d'arts, architecture and photography — that have caught the attention of even the most blasé of visitors. The average museum-goer knows Carpeaux and Rodin, of course, but under the vast vaulting of the Musée d'Orsay he finds himself confronted for the first time with others' works. As for the objets d'art that were tucked away in quiet corners of the Louvre and the Palais de Tokyo, they suddenly have taken on new life and vigour, so much so that visitors are delighted to come upon the furniture rooms, even though these recreations may at times leave something to be desired. Rare for France, there are also entire sections devoted to architectural drawings and models. And even though, for amateurs, photography may play too modest a role, the museum does nevertheless organize temporary exibitions. Other disciplines, like history, literature, music and the cinema, are welcome, too, at the Musée d'Orsay, for the museum wants to present as complete a panorama as possible of the artistic creation of the 19th century. This was made quite clear in the museum programme made public in 1978, and reconfirmed in 1981.

The Musée d'Orsay can be seen in three different ways. Most visitors are happy to follow the rigorous chronological path traced by Gae Aulenti, along

Jean-Paul Laurence,
*L'excommunication
de Robert le Pieux,*
1875, oil on canvas.

DECORATIVE ARTS

Thanks to a large number of acquisitions since 1977, the Musée d'Orsay is one of the rare museums to offer visitors a broad panorama of the decorative arts during the second half of the 19th century and the early years of the 20th century, not only in France but in the principal artistic centres of Europe and the United States.

The solution of period rooms that artificially recreate the atmosphere of a given time was discarded, as was a grouping of objects according to type or technique. It was decided instead to choose works that exemplify a period, be they prototypes for a series or a single object, and which illustrate the intense creative links with the Industrial Revolution. Several rooms are devoted to early attempts to tie Art to Industry, which date back to the first Expositions Universelles. Architects, sculptors, painters and ornamenters created models for manufacturers that had daring combinations of forms and materials, using motifs that were borrowed from earlier styles or that were deliberately exotic. Other works illustrate the Arts and Crafts movement born in England, which tried to create a new aesthetic for modern times.

Nine rooms and two towers are set aside for Art Nouveau, an international movement that flourished at the turn of the century and that tried to bury the styles of the past and begin again from scratch. In addition to such outstanding objects as faience pieces by Gallé, glazed earthenware by Carriès, enamels by Armand Point and Lalique, and stained glass by Gruber or glass creations by Tiffany, the museum boasts an exceptionally fine collection of furniture and decorative elements by some of the best architects, including Horta, Guimard, Van de Velde, Behrens, Mackintosh, Hoffmann and Frank Lloyd Wright. Though it went under different names around the world, Art Nouveau was an international movement that attempted to create a unifying, functional style.

Marc Bascou, Curator.

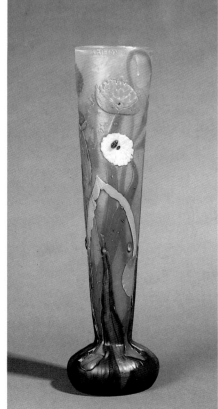

René Lalique, pendant with chain, around 1903-1905, gold, enamel, brilliants, aquamarine.

Morris and Co., after a drawing by Philip Webb, buffet around 1880, mahogany with black finish, partially painted and gilded, painted and varnished embossed leather.

Emile Gallé, *Par une Telle Nuit*, cup, 1894, three layered blown crystal, inclusions of metal paricles, chased and partially gilded decoration.

MUSIC

One of the underlying aims of the organizers of the Musée d'Orsay was to highlight the relationship between music and the other arts of the 1848-1914 period. Music is represented in the exhibits themselves with a room-sized model of the Opera House designed by Garnier, a small room to illustrate the birth of the phonograph and its ties with the cinema, as well as a number of temporary exhibitions. There are also some 30-odd musical events organized each season, including piano and chamber music concerts that feature young as well as confirmed musicians and singers. The music can be part of the usual concert repertory or little known compositions. The museum also organizes workshop concerts, a half-way house between a lecture and a concert, designed for children and youths as well as for adults. In the restaurant, the old tradition of a Sunday afternoon pop concert has been revived. Jean-Michel Nectoux, Curator.

Edgar Degas, *L'Orchestre de l'Opéra*, around 1868-1869, oil on canvas.

The reception room © Couturier/ Archipress.

which they can find all the masterpieces that they have come to admire. Those who are more curious will stop, of course, in front of Manet's *Olympia*, but also in front of the didatic showcases along the way. For those who are passionately interested in the 19th century, there are special exhibitions on a particular theme, concerts and lectures, or old films. Like a few other major museums in the world, there is always something going on at the Musée d'Orsay.

Unlike most museums, it is devoted to a limited period in time, which prompts us to question the faithfulness of the overall picture it presents. Obviously, the picture will never be absolutely complete, and there are still many areas that could be mined more deeply. Even so, the highly developed museological formula may conceal an unsuspected trap: it tends to make us think that everything there is to say has been said and that the picture presented by the museum is the definitive view the 20th century should have of its predecessor. **Laurence Madeline**

The image of perfection according to Ingres, ''La Source'' was 35 years in the making, from 1820 to 1856.

Jean-Dominique Ingres, *La Source*, oil on canvas, 1856.

ING REALITY

The February 1848 Revolution brought in its wake the Second Republic, that was destined to be short-lived. But during the early months, Socialist and Republican ideology was the order of the day, even in the arts. The provisional government let artists take part in their plans for a better society, in particular by organizing a competition for a symbolic representation of the Republic. (The modern concept of the ideologically committed artist may date from that time.)

Be that as it may, the year 1848 constituted a turning point: a number of artists, seeing the profound changes taking place around them, refuted the Romantic notion of art for art's sake and decided to take their subjects from reality. The norms laid down by the Establishment, such as the Academy, were felt to be superfluous. One result was that in the name of equality, the jury was done away with at the 1848 Salon. (The result was a show that had the best, but also the worst, works of art.)

Another sign of the times was the rise of a new school of painting at Barbizon and Chailly, two villages bordering the forest of Fontainebleau. The first artist to set up his easel there was Rousseau, who was soon followed by Dupré, Daubigny, Troyon, and Diaz de la Pena. They all wanted to break away from the iron rule of the Academy; implicit in their vision, which was basically that of the 1848 Revolution, that is, humanistic and slightly sentimental, was their need to work from nature. Canvases like Rousseau's *La Mare, Ciel Orageux*, done around 1860, have nothing anecdotal about them; their only subject is the artist's emotions.

Another proponent of painting out of doors was Camille Corot, who refused to accept the dictates of the Academy any longer. The year 1850 corresponds to Corot's second manner, as diffuse and misty as the light of the Ile de France region. Contrary to the Barbizon painters, he moved away from Realism, which had guided his work till then, and his subsequent landscapes evoked a silent, unreal world (*Une Matinée, Danse des Nymphes*, 1850).

The humanist spirit of 1848 is most apparent in the work of Jean-François Millet. He initially went to Barbizon to flee a cholera epidemic in Paris but ended up living there permanently. Himself the son of peasants, Millet was originally a portrait-painter, but in Barbizon began to depict the peasants around him. He portrayed them as if they were moulded of the same earth they were working. In his paintings, Millet gives them an intemporal, noble quality, and their austere way of life, on the brink of dire poverty, is rendered in dull, earthy tones. Like the people he painted, Millet had a difficult life. Recognition was posthumous, as *The Reapers* (1857) and the *Angelus* (1858-1859) became world famous only after his death.

The manifesto of Realist painting was Gustave Courbet's *Enterrement à Ornans* (1849-1850), in which the artist used a format usually reserved for historical paintings to render a scene from village life. During the 1855 Exposition Universelle in Paris, he clearly affirmed the existence of a new trend in painting by calling the wooden building where he was showing 40 of his canvases, including the important *Atelier*, as the "Realism Pavilion". It is true that many of his still lifes, landscapes, nudes and portraits are bathed in a peaceful, realistic atmosphere, but his large compositions, peopled with strangely silent figures, are more dreamlike than real.

The other outstanding representative of Realism was Honoré Daumier. A late-comer to painting, his beginnings as a cartoonist taught him to strip off the masks people try to hide behind, and his talents as a sculptor can be seen in the powerful, expressionistic rendering of his figures. Though there are still some Romantic reminiscences in his choice of subject-matter, his work as a whole is marked by Realism, and figures like *La Blanchisseuse* (1863) capture the universal qualities of his contemporaries.

Realism also had its official version, which was accepted at the Salons and even won prizes. A number of works illustrated scenes that plucked the heart-

Honoré Daumier, *La Blanchisseuse*, oil on wood, around 1863.

strings of a public taken with sentimental novels and melodramic plays: such as the case of Alexandre Antigna's *L'Eclair* (1848) or Octave Tassert's *La Famille Malheureuse* (1849). Religious scenes, such as Isidore Pil's *Mort d'une Sœur de Charité* (1850), were also very popular.

Industrialisation was making headway, and society was slowly breaking with it peasant background, Jules Breton's *Rappel des Glaneuses* (1859) or Rosa Bonheur's *Labourage Nivernais* (1849), with their anecdotal, bucolic qualities, were still most welcome, unlike Courbet's or Millet's stark representations. While Realism was controversial and divided into different trends, the leading lights of the artistic scene continued to be Ingres and Delacroix, who belonged to the preceding generation. Ingres gave into his passion for the female body one last time with *La Source* (1856), while Delacroix once again evoked his memories of North Africa with *La Chasse aux Lions* (1854) or undertook outsized mural paintings like *Lutte de Jacob et de l'Ange* in the Church of Saint-Sulpice. The retrospectives devoted to their works at the 1855 Exposition Universelle consecrated them as major painters.

That was not so surprising when one remembers that historical and mythological paintings still took pride of place, reflecting the tastes of the public that frequented the Salons. In fact, the situation had scarcely changed since the previous century when commissions and recognition were given primarily to artists who did such works. The proper career for painters much younger than Ingres and Delacroix, like Cabanel, Bouguereau, Henner or Regnault, was usually to win a Prix de Rome, which entitled them to sojourn at the Villa Medicis in Rome, then to become a professor at the School of Fine Arts in Paris and finally to win a seat at the Academy. Subject-matter was taken from ancient Greek and Roman mythology, from the Bible, or from ancient, modern or contemporary history. Technically, these painters were irreproachable, if not virtuosos; their brush-strokes recalled those of the old Venetian or Spanish

Breton's ''Les Glaneuses'', straight as the canephoroi of Antiquity, won him a first-class medal at the 1859 Paris Exposition and was bought by the State. Two years before, Millet had presented his now world-famous version of the same subject. At the time, his less classical rendering was severely criticized. Millet painted a series of lanscapes imbued with a certain symbolism, as can be seen in the Four Seasons series.
Jules Breton, *Le Rappel des Glaneuses*, oil on canvas, 1859.
Jean-François Millet, *Les Glaneuses*, oil on canvas, 1857.
Le Printemps, oil on canvas, 1868-1873.

Admirers of Realism never forgave Courbet for painting ''l'Atelier'' after ''l'Enterrement''. In ''l'Enterrement'' the artist postulated such basic principles as the veracity of the scene observed, as well as borrowings from folk art, to create a long, seemingly naive frieze of people from his native village. He portrayed them paying a last hommage to death. But in the autobiographical ''l'Atelier'', the painter reverted to allegory, showing his private life in the centre. Courbet gravely offered up a hymn to painting: he made references to his masters Rembrandt and Velasquez, he did virtuoso pieces, and for the Paris Exposition, did a canvas with universalistic tendencies. Now that both works are hung together at the Musée d'Orsay, the artist's dream is complete. Courbet was a master painter who wanted to give fresh impetus to the art of his time.

Un Enterrement à Ornans, oil on canvas, 1850.

Shadows dance in the half-light of the artist's studio. The painter finds inspiration in the sky of his native region, the creamy skin of his beloved, or the innocent face of a child. A shawl glows with colour. The painter stands at the centre of the canvas; like a window that opens onto the countryside, a landscape comes to life under his brush. A woman and child, the artist's family, real or allegorical, look on.
L'Atelier, oil on canvas, 1855.

masters, which went to justify their fame and their high prices. Later dubbed *pompiers* (as in "pomp" as well as "pompous"), these painters were an eclectic bunch, ranging from the brilliant Romantic painter Thomas Couture to the meticulous William Bouguereau.

By the early 1860s, the situation was apparently stable but in the space of just a few years, a group of young painters was to push beyond the traditional boundaries of painting to invent modern art.

A leader in this adventure was Edouard Manet, the son of a well-to-do family. He studied painting at Couture's studio, but it was at the Louvre that he copied paintings by Franz Hals and Velasquez and developed his own distinctive style of juxtaposing colours with very few gradations. In 1863 he presented a large canvas at the Salon des Refusés, which Napoléon III had established for those who were being refused permission to show at the official Salon. The canvas in question, originally entitled *Le Bain* and later renamed *Le Déjeuner sur l'Herbe*, created a furor. Two years later, his *Olympia* was accepted at the Salon, but it too proved disturbing to the public.

The Second Empire public saw only obscenity in Manet's works. It was incapable of seeing the similarity in subject-matter and sumptuous technique between his canvases and those of such recognised masters of the past as Georgione, Raphael, Velasquez and Goya. Manet's choice of contemporary subjects was in fact merely a pretext to paint, but in so doing, he broke with the anecdotal tradition of his immediate predecessors. What he also did was to open the way for modern painting.

By dint of scandal, Manet had become the talk of the town, and he soon became the head of a group of young painters, comprised of Renoir, Monet, Sisley and Bazille, who had been working at Gleyre's studio and who were all looking for a new way to go beyond the boundaries of academic painting.

As can be seen in a later painting by Fantin-Latour, called *Un Atelier aux Batignolles* (1870), the young painters gathered round Manet in his studio or in a nearby café called the Café Guerbois, also frequent-

REALISM'S OPPOSITE

The 1848 Revolution constituted a rude awakening for a number of French artists, who suddenly became interested in their own period and realized that it was important to capture its multifarious aspects in painting. But many others were content to continue to depict the gods and heroes that had been portrayed in art ever since the 15th century, a tradition that was to be perpetuated throughout the 19th century. The artists, so as not to be excluded from the annual Salon, continued to treat classical scenes. Moreover, buyers were more readily attracted to subjects that they were used to admiring in the Louvre, rather than people they passed by in the streets each day. Museum pieces thus remained the reference point for artists and collectors alike.

William Bouguereau, *La Naissance de Vénus*, oil on canvas, 1874.

Thomas Couture, *Les Romains de la Décadence*, oil on canvas, 1847.

Even more than painters, sculptors have to rely on commissions. This no doubt explains why subject-matter evolved so little throughout the 19th century. Hippolyte Moulin, *Secret d'en Haut*, marble, 1879.

''*The goddess, drowned in a river of milk, looked like an appetizing woman of easy virtue made not of flesh and blood (that would have been indecent) but of a sort of pink and white almond paste,*'' *wrote Emile Zola.*
Alexandre Cabanel, *La Naissance de Vénus*, oil on canvas, 1863.

ed by Pissarro, Degas and Cézanne.

A contemporary of Manet's and like him of a well-to-do family, Edgar Degas developed his own personal style by studying and copying masters of the past, both in Paris museums and in Italy. His first works show he was familiar with such portrait-painters of the Renaissance as Holbein and Clouet, as can be seen in the *Belleli Family* painted between 1858-1860, or the fresco-painters of the Quattrocento, as seen in *Semiramis Construisant Babylone* (1861). But he was quick to pick up the discoveries of his time, learning lessons in cropping from photography and asymmetrical composition from Japanese prints, which he put to use in canvases with contemporary subject-matter, as in *L'Orchestre de l'Opéra* (1868-1869).

During the 1860s, one of the most pressing problems the younger generation wanted to solve was how to render natural light and figures out of doors. Degas did a series at the race track (*Devant la Tribune*, 1869-1872). Following in the footsteps of Boudin and Jongkind, who experimented with light at the beaches and ports of Normandy a few years earlier, Renoir, Bazille, Monet and Sisley also used the gains made by realist painters like Courbet and the Barbizon School. Monet and Bazille were the first to paint out of doors, having taken living quarters at Chailly, on the edge of Fontainebleau forest. Then in 1865-1866, Monet created his own *Déjeuner sur l'Herbe*; its natural lighting stood in contrast to the abstract light of Manet's work. In 1867 the jury of the Salon refused his *Femmes au Jardin*; that same year, Bazille painted *Réunion de Famille*, in which he, too, tried to solve the problems posed by light and shadow.

The experiments with outdoor light done by Monet in 1869 marks the birth of new kind of painting: like the canvases done by Renoir during the summer at La Grenouillère, on the banks of the Seine, Monet's *Magpie* with its blue-tinged snow announces the coming of Impressionism.

Modern trends had more difficulty coming to the fore in sculpture. Form remained solidly anchored in the past, and neo-classical works continued throughout the century. Leading this field was James Pradier and a group of elegant sculptors known as the "Florentines" because they took their inspiration from the Italian Renaissance; the group included Mercier, Falguière and Moulin. A few sculptors struck out in other directions: among the Romantics were Rude, Préault and Barye; of the handful of Realists, there were Daumier and Meissonier; and above all, there was Jean-Baptiste Carpeaux, a singular genius who took his inspiration from the Renaissance and 18th-century French art to sculpt the figures for the façade of the new Paris Opera house and who succeded in creating sculpture that was at once personal, vital and sensuous.

Philippe Dufour

ORIENTALISM

With his Odalisques, Ingres had merely dreamed of the Orient, but the Romantics actually went there (Decamps left for Turkey in 1828 and Delacroix for North Africa in 1832). Colonical conquests, coupled with the world fairs, had developed peoples' taste for exoticism, and more and more landscape-painters or academic genre painters began to travel to the Orient. They avidly filled their sketchbooks with landscapes and scenes from daily life in the countries they visited. Most of them wanted to discover lifestyles that had not changed since biblical times or Antiquity. Simultaneously, another trend in painting developed in which the Orient was, in fact, only a pretext to depict imaginary or historical scenes that appealed to the perverse or sadistic appetites of the public without arousing the suspicions of the bureau of censorship.

Painting oriental landscapes helped artists discover new colours and new light.

Charles de Tournemine, *Café à Adalia*, in Turkey, oil on canvas, 1861.

Eugène Delacroix, *La Chasse au Tigre*, oil on canvas, 1854.

Here, the painter depicts an imaginary episode in Spanish history. By contrasting the head that has been cut off with the golden splendour of the Alhambra, he is catering to the sadistic instincts of the public.

Henri Regnault, *Exécution Sans Jugement Sous les Rois Maures de Grenade*, oil on canvas, 1870.

TOWN PLANNING DURING THE SECOND EMPIRE

Under the reign of Napoleon III, Paris underwent a radical transformation. It was Baron Haussmann who gave it the look we still know today. It was at this time that the city became a capital that reflected the prosperity of the French nation. Paris was turned into a huge construction site as buildings were torn down to make way for broad boulevards, the Opera house went up and the Louvre was completed. Along with this prestigious building programme, the city was equipped with all the facilities that made for a modern city: a sewerage system and gas lighting, as well as new shops, theatres, markets, parks, schools, hospitals, and apartment buildings designed both for beauty and practicality.

Alphone Crépinet, new Opera house, drawing in perspective, 1861. This project was runner-up in the contest won by Garnier.

Auguste Magne, drawing of the Vaudeville Theatre, elevation of the main façade, 1870.

Monumental door known as a "gallery door" for a private collection or a library; by Fourdinois, 1878, in wood, marble, bronze and enamel.

Jean-Baptiste Carpeaux, *La Danse*; this group of dancing figures was executed in 1869 for the façade of the new Paris Opera house, and was taken down in 1964.

MANET'S ''SCANDALOUS'' WORKS

The year 1863 witnessed, among other things, Cabanel's triumph at the official Salon. His ''La Naissance de Vénus'' won unanimous praise from the jury and was bought by Napoleon III. That very same jury had turned down 3,000 works, which were as a consequence excluded from the official show. To give the public a chance to judge for themselves, the Emperor decided to set up the ''Salon des Refusés'', and it was there that Manet, who was already considered the head of the young school of painting, presented his ''Le Déjeuner sur l'Herbe''. The public had never understood Manet's direct manner in handling modern subjects, but found this particular painting profoundly shocking. By deliberately refusing to depict historical fiction and to idealize his subject, Manet forced his contemporaries to look at the world in a very different way.

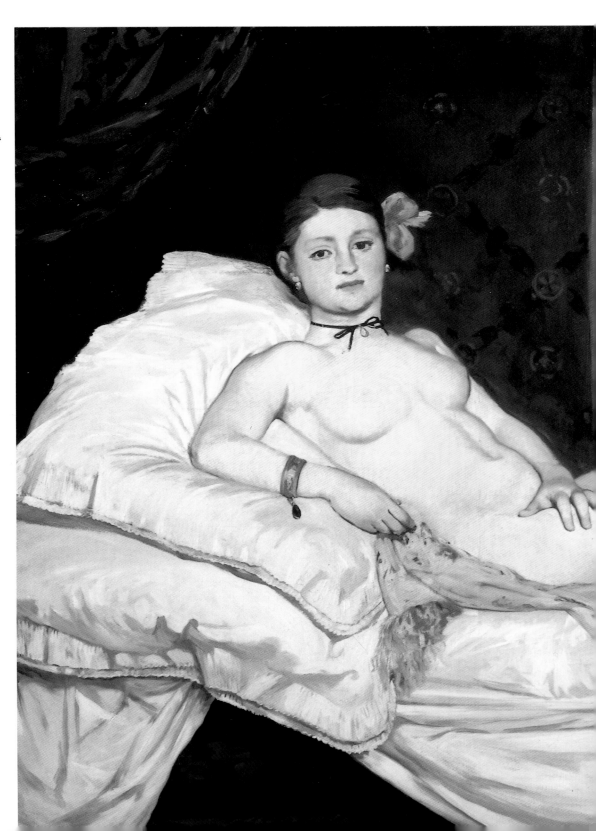

For the journalist and artist Zacharie Astruc, this canvas was the quintessence of art at the Salon des Refusés: "This encapsulates its inspiration, its piquancy, its capacity to astound."
Edouard Manet, *Le Déjeuner sur L'Herbe*, oil on canvas, 1863.

In 1865 Manet provoked another scandal with his "Olympia". What shocked the public at the Salon the most in the work? Was it the direct, cold rendering of the female body? The artist's technique of mixing bright colours with black (the contrast is less strong today)? His simplification of forms? Or was it the rather prudish verses by Astruc that accompanied the canvas, in which the poet referred to the courtesan as "an august young woman whose flame has been dampened"?
Edouard Manet, *L'Olympia*, oil on canvas, 1863.

DECORATIVE ARTS DURING THE SECOND EMPIRE

At every level of society, the eclectic tastes of the period and a love of opulence could be seen in the decorative arts. Like the Imperial family, with its passion for historical styles, people went in for all sorts of ''neo's,'' from neo-Greek and neo-Renaissance to neo-Louis XIV. With the help of sculptors and architects, cabinet-makers were able to produce remarkable works for the world's fairs held in Paris, such as a Merovingian-style medal cabinet by Diehl and Frémiet (1867). Other leading establishments, like Christofle or Barbedienne, created such one-of-a-kind marvels. Only the Emperor or the richest families could afford such magnificent objects, but thanks to the recent marriage of art and industry, even bourgeois families could acquire quality pieces that had been designed by artists and industrially produced.

A second-rate artist with real flair, Carrier-Belleuse helped create the eclectic style of the Second Empire, that lasted well beyond the fall of Napoleon III.
Albert Ernest Carrier-Belleuse (sculptor), Claudius Marioton (tooler), Taxile Doat (ceramicist); made of porphyry, silver, porcelain and black marble, 1886.

This outstanding vase combines forms inspired by the Renaissance with naturalistic motifs; it is a good example of the eclectic mixture of styles so common in the decorative arts during the Second Empire.
Christofle and Co., *Vase de l'Education d'Achille*, glass, gilded silver, 1867.

French history was in fashion during the Second Empire, and even inspired cabinet-makers. Diehl conceived this Merovingian-style medal cabinet for the Paris Exposition of 1867 and asked the sculptor Frémiet for a bas-relief, showing the triumphant entry of Dérovée into Chalons-sur-Marne.
Charles-Guillaume Diehl, E. Brandely, Emmanuel Frémiet, P. Guillemin (sculptors); the cabinet is of cedar, walnut, ebony and ivory, with silver-plated brass and bronze; 1867.

A mix of materials, such as that of wood and pietra dura in Renaissance furniture, corresponded perfectly to the taste for polychrome work during the Second Empire.
Alexandre and Henri Fourdinois, cabinet made of walnut wood, lapis lazuli and jasper, 1867.

EERING DAYS
PRESSIONISM

In the late 1860s, Manet, Renoir, Bazille, Pissarro and Sisley had still not fully realized where they were heading as they experimented with capturing light out of doors. In this respect, the Franco-Prussian War of 1870 was to have a decisive influence, for it forced these artists to go their separate ways. Renoir was called into the army, Bazille was killed at the front, Cézanne moved to the south of France at l'Estaque, while Pissaro and Monet fled the war and poverty in France to take refuge in London, where they hoped to be able to work and sell their paintings. As Pissarro was to confide years later, "We also went to museums... Turner's and Constable's water-colours and paintings certainly influenced us. Their experiments with outdoor scenes, light, and fleeting effects were closer to our own preoccupations."

This discovery precipitated their own evolution. Rain, snow and fog became subjects of study which allowed them to go even further in their observation of light, the rendering of fleeting effects, and the division of colour.

It was also in London that they made a decisive encounter: Daubigny introduced them to the art dealer Durand-Ruel, the same man who had dared to defend Courbet and then Manet. Durand-Ruel took up the banner of this group of contested avant-garde artists, and never failed to give them his unwavering support. This was all the more important because their paintings were generally being turned down by the increasingly adamant juries of the official Salons. This refusal led them to band together to defend their common goals. Monet, Pissarro, Renoir, Berthe Morisot and Sisley, with the support of Degas, founded the "Limited Company of Painters, Sculptors and Engravers", which was set up to organize independent exhibitions without juries or prizes. Manet, who had been the unwilling spokesman for the group ever since the scandal of the 1863 Salon des Refusés, refused to join their company. The salon, he felt, was the "best place to join battle". The first show was held in 1874 in the studios of the photographer Nadar on the Boulevard des Capucines, near the Opera. Thirty artists participated, among them Guillaumin and Cézanne (presented by Pissarro), De Nittis, Legros and Bracquemond (presented by Degas), Boudin and Jongkind, and 165 works were on view. Established art critics were more than ever convinced that these were absurd daubings, and railed against the painters "who have declared war against beauty".

Art critic Louis Leroy joined the chorus, mocking Monet's *Impression, Soleil Levant*: "Impression... I knew it must be something like that. As I'm impressed, there must be some impression somewhere..." The term "Impressionism" became a catchword, and even the artists themselves adopted it, as did their small circle of friends, art critics and collectors (which included Jules Castagnary, Edmond Duranty, Théodore Duret and Georges Rivière).

For the next 12 years, till 1886, seven other exhibitions were organized under the Impressionist banner, and this in spite of bitter attacks from without and squabbling, both personal and aesthetic, from within. Some artists broke away: Cezanne after 1877, Monet, Sisley and Renoir in 1880 ind 1886. But new artists took their place: Gustave Caillebotte in 1876, Mary Cassatt and Gauguin in 1879, and Seurat and Signac in 1886.

During the 1860s the group spent a good deal of time discussing what the term "impression" really involved. "The meetings at the Café Guerbois," commented art critic Théodore Duret, "were very fruitful. Manet contributed his use of lighter colours to painting and Claude Monet, Pissaro and Renoir brought with them the techniques of painting out of doors."

Though they had no aesthetic theory per se, these artists developed a new way of painting because they had found a new way of looking at things, born of immediate sensations. Because the light changed constantly, what they saw also changed continually, and these "fleeting impressions" became the real subject of their paintings, forcing artists to abandon traditional principles. Perspective no longer obeyed the

Auguste Renoir, *La Balançoire*, oil on canvas, 1876.

strict rules of geometry: it was defined instead by a division of colours, just as broken brushstrokes, rather than line, suggested form and volume. Applying the theories of Chevreul (1830) on the chromatic circle and optical mixing, the Impressionists used only primary colours (red, blue and yellow) and complementary colours (orange, violet and green). By juxtaposing them on their canvases, they wanted to render all the vibrating colours in the air. The aim was to capture what hit their retina, at once instants in daily life and the ephemeral aspects of nature.

A large number of canvases, painted prior to 1872-1874, show their common concerns; the same kind of experiments can be seen in particular in the canvases painted in 1869 by Monet and by Renoir at La Grenouillère. Monet's influence became so preponderant that he was soon looked upon as the leader of the group. On his return from England via Holland, Monet settled at Argenteuil in 1871, where he was to stay till 1878. Despite serious financial problems, he worked hard, more often than not using a boat set up as a studio, like Daubigny before him. Tirelessly he sought to capture the effects of light in the sky and on the water, the vibrations set in motion when the sun came out or when clouds turned the sky grey, as in the canvases of boats and regattas on the Seine at Argenteuil. Water fascinated him to such an extent that he once declared: "I would always like to be in it or on it, and when I die, I want to be buried in a life-preserver."

Capturing successive instants of vision, he varied his technique by using broken brushstrokes of bright tones, by dividing colours into their components, and by breaking up surfaces and masses. The canvases painted during this period attest to Monet's exacerbated sensibility and to his growing capacity to render fleeting light effects on the rippled surface of the water, including the unpredictable effects of the wind.

Water was to be one of the major themes of the Impressionists, who came in turn to work with Monet at Argenteuil. As they painted side by side, they would compare notes, measuring their audacity in using

After his series devoted to haystacks and to poplar trees, Monet followed suit with "Cathedrals" (dated 1894 but done between 1892 and 1893). In these different versions of the same subject, he followed the changes in light hour by hour, capturing the "instantaneous" transformations it made on the stone.
Claude Monet, *La Cathédrale de Rouen* (Harmony in blue and gold, Harmony in white, Harmony in blue, Harmony in brown), oil on canvas, 1892-1894.

PAINTING OUT OF DOORS

"We enjoyed the day," wrote the Goncourt brothers, "the fatigue, the speed, the fresh air, the warm sun, its rays darting about on the land. (... We were) drunk with a near-animal joy of being alive on a broad river in beautiful weather and blinding light." These few lines illustrate the radiant vitality born of fresh air that the Impressionist painters tried to convey. Starting in the mid-19th century, the less privileged classes from the capital liked to go up to the Moulin de la Galette in the nearby village of Montmartre, or to the banks of the Seine at Argenteuil, Bougival or Marly, the latter only 20 minutes from the city thanks to the new train to Saint-Germain-en-Laye. There they would enjoy bathing, canoeing, dancing in inexpensive open-air restaurants or picnicking.

Claude Monet, *Femme à l'Ombrelle*, oil on canvas, 1886.

Claude Monet, *Les Coquelicots* (detail), oil on canvas, 1873.

Cézanne succeeds in breaking down the various planes of this landscape by the use of colour masses. Here, he went even further than the Impressionists in his attempt to do away with traditional perspective.
Paul Cézanne, *L'Estaque*, oil on canvas, 1878-1879.

Auguste Renoir,
*Chemin Montant
Dans Les Herbes*
(detail), oil on
canvas, 1878.

This very large canvas is especially interesting for its asymmetrical composition, in the manner of Degas.

Gustave Caillebotte, *Les Raboteurs de Parquet*, oil on canvas, 1875.

colours but keeping their own distinctive styles. Even Manet, who had kept his distance and who had refused to participate in their group shows, turned up at Argenteuil during the summer of 1874. Working out of doors alongside his painter friends was to have a definite effect on his work, for from that point on, his paintings became much more luminous.

Unlike Monet, who worked with broken brushstrokes of contrasting colours to meld together his figures and the surrounding air, Manet wanted to emphasize form, which he did by using more intense colours and by Japanese style asymmetrical composition. Caillebotte's early works, like *Les Raboteurs de Parquet* (1875), were marked by Realism, but Monet's influence can be seen starting in the 1880s, when the artist devoted himself almost exclusively to painting the Seine (like his *Voiliers à Argenteuil*).

Art critic Armand Silvestre was not far off the mark when he wrote in 1874: "Monet is the cleverest and the most daring, Sisley is the most harmonious and the most timid, Pissarro the most realistic and the most naive." No doubt Sisley suffered even more than his friends from poverty and public incomprehension. His canvases reveal a quiet equilibrium born of delicate tones of grey, pink and light green. Typical works are *L'Inondation à Port-Marly*, in which the sky, water and earth become one, and *Neige à Louveciennes*. As for Pissarro, he settled down in Pontoise, some 20 miles from Paris, in 1872, where he painted in the company of Cézanne. Though his harmony of colours and his light brushtrokes show incredible freedom, strong, structured composition serves to anchor his works. Pissarro's preference went to small country villages rather than to water-scapes. He was a true naturelover, and it was only poor health that forced him to leave the country for Paris, where he painted a number of cityscapes, years after Renoir and Monet.

The French capital was the crucible of modern life, and as early as 1872, both Monet and Renoir, used it as the subject of some of their best works. (Monet's "La Rue Montorgueil", 1878.) They succeeded in capturing its fast pace and its special light in dynam-

In this work, Rodin created a figure that throbs with pain and tortured thoughts, showing such mastery that he was accused of having made a plaster cast of a living figure for it. Auguste Renoir, *L'Age d'Airain*, bronze.

In this incomplete canvas, Monet took up one of his favourite subjects, that of reflections of the sky and of objects on water. Claude Monet, *Régates à Argenteuil*, oil on canvas, around 1872.

Here the village blends into the background, and it is the rooftops that attract our attention. As always with Pissarro, the composition is very solid. Camille Pissarro, *Les Toits Rouges*, oil on canvas, 1877.

Degas often liked to portray laundrywomen ironing, which for him was yet another chance to treat movement and capture just the right gesture. Edgar Degas, *Les Repasseuses*, oil on canvas, around 1884-1886.

ON THE SEASIDE

During the course of the 19th century, the railroads opened up entire areas, both to city-dwellers eager to enjoy their leisure time, and to painters, who could discover new subjects for their works. Like the countryside and the forest, the sea was brought closer to Paris, and its image changed. As tourists gradually took over the beaches, the sea began to seem tame, losing its 18th-century connotations of a mysterious and immense stretch of water ever ready to swallow ships. True, some artists still illustrated the romantic, heroic aspects of the sea, as certain works by Courbet and Monet attest, but most painters primarily showed interest in the limitless, ever-changing image of the sea and tried to capture the subtle harmonies of colour between sea and sky.

Unlike Boudin, Manet centres his painting on the two figures sitting on the sand, thereby letting us share their view of the sea and sky. Edouard Manet, *Sur La Plage*, oil on canvas, 1873.

Gustave Courbet, *La Falaise d'Etretat Après l'Orage*, oil on canvas, 1869.

Eugène Boudin, *La Plage de Trouville*, oil on canvas, 1862.

For Monet, a train station was not merely a place to pass through. It was a theme worthy of a painter living in the heroic Machine Age. Claude Monet, *La Gare Saint-Lazare*, oil on canvas, 1877.

ic and daring plunging views, as they looked down from the windows where they had set up their easels. Train stations were another emblem of the modern world that Monet, for one, wanted to capture. He was captivated by the rich possibilities of the subject, with forms that constantly changed because of the steam roiling around the engines. He did a total of seven paintings on the Gare St. Lazare, announcing his subsequent penchant for series on a single subject.

As for Renoir, he applied the principles of Impressionism to his figure paintings and, as he excelled at portrait-painting, he made his livelihood from it. In 1876, Renoir painted three of his most famous canvases: *Le Bal du Moulin de la Galette*, a scene showing working-class couples dancing in a country setting, *La Balançoire* and *Torse de Femme au Soleil*, which critics castigated as a "pile of decomposing flesh." All these works are animated by a play of pink light and blue shadows, that at once hide and reveal forms as rays of sunlight dart through the leaves.

Though Degas was the main organizer of the Impressionist exhibitions, he joined up with these painters not out of common convictions but to defend artistic freedom, to gain recognition and to sell his work. "My art," he claimed, "is anything but spontaneous. What I do is the result of reflexion and the study of the great masters." Rather than paint out of doors, Degas prefered "what one sees in one's memory." To Pissarro, he once explained, "You need natural life, whereas what I need is artificial life." Whether he worked in oils, watercolours or pastels, Degas chose decidedly contemporary subjects: the hubbub of the racetrack (as in *Chevaux de Course Devant Les Tribunes*, around 1879); the magic of singers in popular cafés or dancers at the Opera (*Danseuse au Bouquet Saluant*, 1878); café scenes (*L'Absinthe*, 1876); and lastly, portrayals of laundry-women and milliners. Each time, though, Degas chose to show not the glitter but the hard work taking place behind the scenes. In each case, too, the artist chose to explore movement by breaking down gestures, to experiment with space by using asymmetrical composition and ingenious cropping, and to try new chromatic effects. He succeeded in coupling complete technical mastery with great freedom. In Degas's own words, he was "the classical painter of modern life."

During the "heroic" 1870s, the quality of the Impressionists' work was matched only by the disdain of the critics. But by the end of the decade, when the movement was getting a modicum of recognition, sponteneity was decidedly on the wane. Certain artists in the group, in particular Pissarro and Renoir, were becoming aware of the defects if not the dangers of the movement.

"Around 1883," Renoir confined years later to his dealer Ambroise Vollard, "it was as if something had broken in my work. I had followed Impressionism to its end and had come to the conclusion that I knew neither how to paint nor to draw. In a word, I was at a dead end." The artist nonetheless began to draw again, adopting a linear style reminiscent of Ingres and chose to paint nudes, which he called "an indespensable art form."

Pissarro, who till then had concentrated on landscapes, began to do figures. At the instigation of his young friends Seurat and Signac, he next turned to Divisionism and to Pontillism.

By this time, these various artists who had gone a long way together came to a parting of the ways. They had attained maturity, and each was to follow his own path. Their experience as a group came to a definite end with an eighth and last exhibition, in 1886, which no longer went under the name of "Impressionism." What is more, some of the major figures did not participate in it: Monet, Sisley and Renoir were notable for their absence. What was left for these artists to share was the gradual recognition of art lovers and critics, and at long last of the public at large.

The artists had attained maturity, and each was to follow his own path. Meanwhile, the early 1880s saw the beginnings of a new aesthetic evolution with Seurat, Gauguin, Van Gogh and Toulouse-Lautrec. True, they had been nourished by Impressionism but they then took a stand against it.

Caroline Larroche

The blurred face and torso in this painting indicate that the artist was more interested in studying the reflections of the sun on the model's body.
Auguste Renoir, *Torse de Femme au Soleil*, oil on canvas, 1876.

The daring composition and the contrast of colours point to the influence of Manet, who was the teacher and brother-in-law of Berthe Morisot.
Berthe Morisot, *Le Berceau*, oil on canvas, 1872.

THE WORLD OF ENTERTAINMENT

A number of artists chose such typically modern subjects as those to be found in the world of entertainment and, unlike the Impressionists who liked to paint out of doors, they studied the effects of artificial lighting. Honoré Daumier took the Romantic's view of the theatre, with faces distorted by the violent shadows cast by footlights, as in ''Crispin

''... In the world of dance, there is no place for repose; immobility can only be a constraint,'' noted poet Paul Valéry in ''Degas, Danse, Dessin''.
Edgar Degas, *L'Etoile*, oil on canvas, 1878.

et Scapin''. The elegant Edgar Degas was an ardent music lover who attended the Opera assiduously. He rendered the half-light of the orchestra pit and especially the spiralling light that seemed to sculpt the bodies of ballet dancers on stage, in the wings and during rehearsals. Degas also painted singers in cafés, which came to be one of Henri de Toulouse-Lautrec's most famous subjects. It was he, better than anyone, who rendered the atmosphere of turn-of-the-century Paris music halls and their ephemeral stars, captured for eternity in a few expressive lines (''Jane Avril Dansant'', around 1893).

In this oil painting, Degas succeeds in imparting to the ''Blue Dancers'' all the resonance of pastels, a medium he took to using more and more often during the 1890s to translate the shimmering effects of light.
Edgar Degas, *Danseuses Bleues*, oil on canvas, 1890.

Edgar Degas, *Répétitions d'un ballet sur la scène*, oil on canvas, 1874.

A regular customer at such Parisian cabarets as "Le Moulin Rouge," "Le Rat Mort," "Le Mirliton" or "Le Divan Japonais," Toulouse-Lautrec liked to paint the other regular customers with ferocious exaggeration.
Henri de Toulouse-Lautrec, *Jane Avril Dansant*, oil on cardboard, 1892.

Toulouse-Lautrec, whose physical deformity was caused by a horseback-riding accident, was most likely fascinated by the well-known actor Samary, who strode about the stage of the repertory Comédie Française with great assurance.
Toulouse-Lautrec, *Henry Samary*, oil on cardboard, 1889.

Conceived as a pair, these two paintings have almost always been shown together since the first exhibition in 1883, at the Galerie Durand-Ruel. The straightforward composition and the way the figures stand out clearly against the background point to Renoir's renewed interest in drawing in the 1880s.
Auguste Renoir, *Danse à la Ville, Danse à la Campagne*, oil on canvas, 1882-1883.

Renoir was a regular customer at the Moulin de la Galette, where Parisians liked to come to dance in a country setting. This large work was done on the premises.
Auguste Renoir, *Le Bal du Moulin de la Galette*, oil on canvas, 1876.

IMPRESSIONISM PUSHED TO ITS LIMITS

Around 1886, Renoir declared that he had gone as far as he could with Impressionism and that for a time he was going to reconstruct his work by drawing. Thirty years later, he felt he was ready to push his Impressionist technique even further and did so by deliberately melding forms into a stream of colour. Even so, the figures are still clearly visible. At Giverny, Monet, too, tried to push Impressionism to its logical conclusion. The pioneer of Impressionism often had trouble making out the forms and colours of the water lilies in his pond. He scrutinized them so carefully that the real world, which was after all at the heart of his concerns, all but disappeared. As Monet took more and more liberties with his paintings, the subject can only be guessed at. In the explosion of colour that marks his ''Nymphéas'' series it seems evident that Monet was moving towards abstraction.

Monet created two different types of garden at Giverny, one of earth, the other of water. It was during the last years of his life that he worked intensively on the water-lily pond, as if were hypnotised by the small stretch of water with brightly coloured flowers scattered over its surface. He wrote to his friend Geffroy: ''You should know that I am absorbed by my work. These waterscapes and reflections have become an obsession. It is more than I can handle, but I nonetheless want to succeed in rendering what I feel.''
Claude Monet, *Nymphéas Bleus*, oil on canvas.

Renoir painted his "Baigneuses" in a state of elation and considered it as "a culmination," according to his son Jean Renoir. "He felt he had synthesized the experiments of a lifetime and had laid the groundwork for his future work." Auguste Renoir, *Les Baigneuses*, oil on canvas, 1918-1919.

THE FAD FOR JAPAN

During the second half of the 19th century, Japanese art and aesthetics were all the rage. This was a direct result of the opening up of Japan to international trade in 1853 and its subsequent participation in the Paris Expositions, where Japanese objects were on view and sometimes up for sale. Intellectuals like the Goncourt brothers and Emile Zola, and artists like Manet, Degas, Whistler and Van Gogh began to collect Japanese objects: ivory, cloisonné enamel, lacquer work, porcelain and embroidery. Over and beyond their exotic appeal, avant-garde artists found matter for thought in these prints. In their search for a more modern approach to art, they were intrigued by the way Japanese artists handled everyday subjects, their unusual composition and their new way of handling flat areas of colour. It at once constituted a fresh approach to and a justification for their own experiments. The implications of Japanese art meant a simplification of means, naturalist observation, more refined colours and asymmetrical composition.

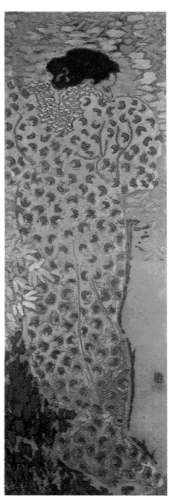

Bonnard's handling of forms and colours, the elongated format and the support similar to a Japanese scroll are ample evidence of the Japanese influence on his work. Indeed, Bonnard was nicknamed the "Very Japanese Nabi".
Pierre Bonnard, *Le Peignoir*, oil on cloth, 1892.

Eugène Rousseau plays on the transparency of his material to heighten the naturalistic rendering of this carp motif, a direct borrowing from a Japanese model.
Eugène Rousseau, vase, around 1878, of glass with chased and painted decoration and incrustations.

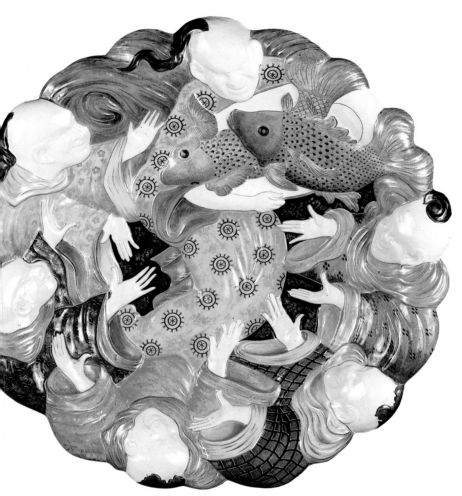

This ornamental platter is a highly personal synthesis of Japanese, Chinese and Renaissance influences.
Emile Gallé, ornamental platter in faience, polychrome decoration on stanniferous enamel, ivory and gold accents, around 1878.

Console table with cupboard serves to set off a panel painted by Detaille. The representation of a Japanese warrior more closely resembles Chinese than Japanese style.
Edouard Lièvre, a set of two pieces of furniture (cupboard on console table).

Gauguin portrayed his models from close up, like a photographic snapshot; this gives the painting a monumental feeling that contrasts with the simplicity of the subject.
Paul Gauguin, *Femmes de Tahiti* or *Sur La Plage*, oil on canvas, 1891.

OOMING OF NEW TRENDS

The year 1886 marked a turning point, if not a break-off point, in the history of French painting. It was the year that the Impressionists held their last group show together and that new artists began to question the recent advances in painting. For two years the Neo-Impressionists, inspired in part by Seurat's *Une Baignade, Asnières* (Tate Gallery, London), developed their ideas and in 1886 they constituted their own movement at the second Salon des Indépendants. That same year the Symbolist manifesto was published. Though it dealt primarily with poetry and fiction, its spirit soon affected the visual arts as well. Indeed, one of the reasons why Paris was the art centre of the world at the turn of the century, was the close relations that existed between writers and painters. Van Gogh had gone to Paris precisely with the intention of coming into contact with the intellectual effervescence of the French capital. It was there that he made friends with Signac, Emile Bernard, Toulouse-Lautrec and Gauguin. Of the major painters, only Cézanne stood apart, as he lived and worked in Aix-en-Provence, in the south of France. Unlike the Impressionists, the Neo-Impressionists wanted to rigorously apply the results of optical research, even though they still used similar subjects: seascapes and views of the Seine, scenes from daily life, and portraits.

As art critic Félix Fénéon, pointed out, Seurat innovated by practising Divisionism: "Instead of mixing colours on his palette which, once put on the canvas, would approximate the colour of the object being represented, the artist placed brushstrokes that corresponded to the local colour of the object, others that corresponded to reflections cast by adjacent objects, and still others representing the complementaries of the overall light." This seemingly purely technical reform, based on the scientific writings of Chevreul, in fact implied an overall revision of current artistic thinking. However, it would be a mistake to think that Neo-Impressionism was intended merely as a rigorous application of a scientific theory; Seurat hoped to elicit an emotional response from his visual play of lines and colours.

Shortly after the birth of Neo-Impressionism, Jean Moréas signed a manifesto in the September 1886 literary supplement of *Le Figaro* which signalled the birth of Symbolism. Unlike other movements at the time, no mode of expression was preferred over another. In the words of the poet Verlaine: "There are as many symbols as there are Symbolists." Symbolists wanted to give reign to ideas; according to one definition, Symbolism was meant "to tell the onlooker something; like poetry, to give him something to think about; or like a piece of music, to transmit an impression."

The Symbolists refused the brutal transformations that were taking place around them and vaunted the values which they sensed would soon be lost. A number of them, like Moreau, Gauguin and Redon, took refuge in the mystical or imaginary worlds they created, while others, like Carrière or Camille Claudel, took their inspiration from their own lives.

One of the principle initiators of the movement was Paul Gauguin (1848-1903). He had previously worked in the Impressionist style, taking his inspiration for his portraits and landscapes from Degas and Pissarro. Though he had exhibited with the Impressionists from 1879 to 1886, he had attracted little attention. Leaving off with the broken brushstrokes of his first, Impressionist period (*Nature Morte à la Mandoline*, 1885), Gauguin began to use colour so subjectively that it at times no longer corresponded at all to objective reality. To this, he added a highly original sense of composition. In the half-length portrait of *La Belle Angèle* (1889), the figure is separated from the background by a half-circle that recalls a Japanese hair-frame. The Peruvian-looking anthropomorphic ceramic pieces placed in front of a decorative landscape indicate the symbolic intentions that Gauguin wanted to impart to his portrait-painting.

In the Breton village of Pont-Aven, where he went to stay a second time in 1888, Gauguin brought to fruition the experiments of the preceding two years.

Paul Gauguin, *Le Cheval Blanc*, oil on canvas, 1898.

Gauguin painted the ancient necropolis of Alycamps during his stay with Van Gogh during the winter of 1888. The stick-like brushtrokes and strong colours suffice to render the unforgettable atmosphere of the place.
Paul Gauguin, *Les Alycamps*, oil on canvas, 1888.

In close collaboration with Emile Bernard, he elaborated the theory of Synthetism or Cloisonnism, which he later developed fully in Tahiti, and which Paul Sérusier was to teach to the Nabis. In Synthetism, forms are simplified, colours are applied flat and cover fairly large areas, and traditional Western perspective is replaced by daring asymmetrical composition reminiscent of Japanese prints.

Many artists had been going to Brittany ever since the 1860s, where they found "nature devoid of any trace of modern life, where Druid, Catholic and feudal ruins are scattered about the countryside like so many loose pages of a forgotten history book." Gauguin, who had spent part of his chilhood in Peru, found it "wild and primitive". As he wrote to his friend Schuffenecker, "My wooden shoes make the same dull, powerful sound that I want to create in my paintings."

Tahiti was to be the last stage in Gauguin's quest for primitive religious sentiment. The paintings done during the last 20 years of his life were devoted to developing Synthetism (*Femmes de Tahiti*, 1891; *Arearea*, 1892; *Le Cheval Blanc*, 1898). His interest in native rites led him to create what Octave Mirbeau called in 1891, "a disquieting mixture of barbarian splendour, Catholic liturgy, Hindu dreams, Gothic imagery, and subtle, obscure symbolism".

In direct response to the aesthetics proned by Gauguin, the Nabi group (from the Hebrew word for prophet) was formed in 1890, shortly after Paul Sérusier did his *Talisman*, a rapidly executed work with a totally free use of colours, done under the supervision of the "Master of Pont-Aven". The Nabis were a kind of congenial fraternity that included Maurice Denis, Sérusier, Bonnard, Vuillard and Ranson, among others. Like Gauguin, they were above all interested in a painter's freedom: "The principal subject," wrote Bonnard towards the end of his life, "is the surface, which has colours and laws that go beyond the (objects) painted." The Nabis as a group were ready to dare anything and had no time for such conventions as traditional perspective, preferring

Unlike the Impressionists with their intuitive perception of forms and colours, Cézanne took a more rational attitude based on the geometrical treatment of volumes.
Paul Cézanne, *La Femme à la Cafetière*, oil on canvas, 1890-1895.

During his first stay in Pont-Aven in 1886, Paul Gauguin was still painting in the Impressionist manner, as can be seen in ''Les Lavandières à Pont-Aven''. It was only two years later, on his return from Martinique, that the artist, in collaboration with Emile Bernard, elaborated the theories for Cloisonnism, the first stage of Synthetism. Scenes of the unchanging, austere life in Brittany answered Gauguin's need for formal primitivism. He was also attracted by the Bretons' spirituality, and his canvases give off a mystic sense; the heavy outlines surrounding areas of flat colour recall stained-glass windows. Gauguin and Bernard attracted a group of enthusiastic artists, including Laval, Moret, Schuffenecker, Maufra, Verkade and Sérusier, who put their lessons into practice. In 1889, the group exhibited their works in Paris at the Café Volpini, astounding the art critics of the time.

After having worked closely together in 1888, Gauguin and Bernard went their separate ways. Under the initial shock of his discovery of Oceania in 1891, Gauguin painted figures that looked like primitive idols, whereas Bernard developed a more geometrical style, in which Cézanne's influence can be seen.
Paul Gauguin, *Paysannes Bretonnes*, oil on canvas, 1894.
Emile Bernard, *La Moisson Au Bord de la Mer*, oil on canvas, 1891.

Paul Sérusier, *Le Talisman*, oil on canvas, 1888.

In "Sudden Shower", Sérusier applied the lessons of the School of Pont-Aven. The composition, on the other hand, is asymmetrical, inspired by Japanese prints, while the collage of superimposed planes is reminiscent of the Nabis.
Paul Sérusier, *L'Averse* (detail), egg-based paint on canvas, 1892-1895.

Japanese-style composition instead. What varied was their subject-matter: Denis's mysticism is apparent in *La Montée au Calvaire* (1889), while Vuillard's intimism can be seen in *Au Lit* (1891). Like the English pre-Raphaelites, they wanted to bring poetry into daily life. Without exception, they all cried "Walls, give us walls to decorate".

When Van Gogh (1853-1890) arrived in Paris, his first paintings recalled the realistic portraits and country scenes done in his native Holland; in La Guinguette (1886), he used dark colours to depict the little restaurant near Montmartre. But his style quickly changed as he discovered the latest artistic trends and met other painters at the Cormon studio or at Pere Tanguy's paint shop. From the Impressionists, he learned to use pure, bright colours and took to painting such working-class places as *Le Restaurant à Asnières* (1887). With Paul Signac, he tried his hand at Neo-Impressionistic landscapes in the suburbs of Paris, but instead of using rigorous technique for its own sake, he put it to decorative use, as in *Nature Morte Aux Fritillaires* (1887). He was so taken with strong colours and with Japanese prints that he decided to go to Provence, where he thought he would find landscapes similar to those in Japan. Interested by the solutions proposed by Gauguin and Emile Bernard, he became aware of the expressive powers of colour. "Things here have so much line," Van Gogh wrote his brother Theo, "and I want to get my drawing more spontaneous, more exaggerated." *La Salle de Danse à Arles* (1888) is strongly influenced by Synthetism: with forms surrounded by a thick black line and with violent colours applied flat, the work verges on caricature.

Van Gogh continued to paint during his internment in the insane asylum at Saint-Rémy-de-Provence, though his colours turned darker in his search for a more "male" line. At Auvers-sur-Oise, he did a number of portraits, including *Le Portrait du Docteur Gachet* (1890), which he himself called "apparitions". In the same year, his visionary *L'Eglise d'Auvers* took

Cézanne did five different versions of these card players, each time reducing the number of players as he searched for the optimum use of space.
Paul Cézanne, *Les Joueurs de Cartes*, oil on canvas, 1890-1895.

Bonnard here shows his family in the garden. Their game of croquet is a pretext to do a large-sized study comprised of supple silhouettes.
Pierre Bonnard, *La Partie de Croquet*, oil on canvas, 1892.

PORTRAITURE

For centuries, the art of portrait-painting was subject to certain rules: a portrait had to be a good likeness and had to be technically proficient. But with the invention of photography and the new possibilities it offered, portraiture underwent major changes. The biggest innovation was to be found in the affirmation of certain aesthetic intentions. It was a way for the artist, through the study of his model, to give his own interpretation of society, as well as a pretext to come up with new pictorial solutions. Apparently, all the portrait-painters of the period, especially during the last three decades of the century, came round to this new approach. There were any number of daring experiments, and rarely before had models been rendered with such expressiveness.

Vincent van Gogh,
*Le Docteur Paul
Gachet*, oil on
canvas, 1890.

Paul Gauguin, *La Belle Angèle*, oil on canvas, 1889.

Edouard Manet, *Le Balcon* (detail, portrait of Berthe Morisot), oil on canvas, 1868-1869.

Eugène Carrière (1849-1906), *Alphonse Daudet et Sa Fille*, oil on canvas, 1891.

Degas painted this group portrait in Florence at the home of his aunt, Baroness Laure Bellelli. It reveals Degas' acute eye for psychological traits, heightened by an unusual composition. Edgar Degas, *La Famille Bellelli*, oil on canvas, 1858-1860.

Félix Tournachon, called Nadar, *Baudelaire*, print on salted paper, from a glass negative with wet collodion.

65

on a tragic, premonitory dimension.

Among the painters whom Van Gogh had met on arriving in Paris, only four short years before he committed suicide, was Toulouse-Lautrec (1864-1901). The latter settled in Montmartre and soon became a passionate chronicler of music halls and brothels. It was there that he slowly built up his "Olympus," which included, among others, the song-writer Aristide Bruant, dancer Jane Avril and singer Yvette Guilbert. He would have remained a mere chronicler had it not been for his sharp eye for psychological traits and the sureness of his drawing. Often painted on pieces of cardboard, his scenes were like snapshots executed with exceptional directness, which he succeeded in transposing in his posters thanks to his use of flat colours and stylised drawing.

During his youth, when he was still a provincial painter with few contacts in Paris, Paul Cézanne (1839-1906) produced some highly personal, baroque works that seem like so many tardy outcroppings of Romanticism. Typical of this period is the *Portrait d'Achille Emperaire* (1868-1870), with its dark colours applied in thick daubs and its expressive distortions. Cézanne was briefly attracted to the Impressionists' experiments, both technically and aesthetically. Working with Pissarro, he gave up the complex subject-matter of his earlier works as well as *chiaroscuro* inspired by 17th-century Italian art. By working on his subject directly, he began to use brighter colours, but by 1873 with *La Maison du Pendu*, his almost uniform use of a greyish-green and his desire to build a coherent composition herald his mature style. The artist's frequent stays at Jas-du-Buffon, his home near Aix, helped him along. In *L'Estaque* (1878-1879), parallel brushstrokes, the geometric-looking forms and the use of linear perspective to suggest depth all go to create his intellectual representation of space. Its logic cuts across traditional boundaries; thus, the portrait of *La Femme à La Cafetière* (1890-1895), which is treated like a landscape or a still life, is a strict implementation of the artist's famous declaration: "Treat nature through cyclinders, spheres

Vincent van Gogh, *L'Arlésienne*, oil on canvas, 1888.

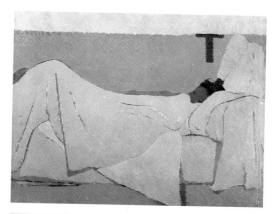

This work by Vuillard is an excellent illustration of Maurice Denis's definition of painting: apart from any consideration of subject-matter, a painting is above all "a flat surface coverd with colours assembled in a certain order." Edouard Vuillard, *Au lit*, oil on canvas, 1891.

Like the Nabis, Vuillard was very interested in mural decorations. A set of nine paintings called "Les Jardins Publics", of which the Musée d'Orsay has five, was originally done for the town house of Alexandre Natanson. Edouard Vuillard, *Les Jardins publics* (détail).

Vallotton was part of the Nabi circle and applied himself to painting large areas of flat colour and simplified forms. Félix Vallotton.

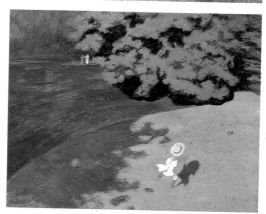

and cones.'' But colour harmony is the point at which rigorous construction and visual emotion meet. In *Nature Morte aux Pommes et Oranges* (1890-1895), there are only a few yellow-orangy and grey-green tones, but they are used with such intelligence that they create the relief and the light specific to each object.

Though Gauguin, Van Gogh and Cézanne were still considered marginal artists by Establishment critics on the eve of the 20th century, they had, in fact, laid the foundations for a new approach to painting. For the coming generations, a return to primitivism and to pure colours, as well as a new sense of composition, were to be the order of the day.

The last rooms of the Musée d'Orsay are devoted to Fauvism, which in a way highlights the ambivalence of this short-lived movement. Some of the most vital trends of late 19th-century art came together in Fauvism, and the Fauves' preoccupations made it an art form that heralded future trends.

Almost all the artists who were to become known as the Fauves had worked in the studio of Gustave Moreau, where they learned about the "necessary richness of colour". What is more, Van Gogh's use of colour was to prove a revelation when his works where shown at the Galerie Bernheim in 1901. To paint his *Luxe, Calme et Volupté*, Matisse worked alongside Signac during the summer of 1904. These various experiences set off the dynamics of colour which became the basis for the Fauvist movement. Brought together for the first time at the 1905 Salon d'Automne by Matisse, the principal proponents of Fauvism, Derain, Vlaminck, Marquet, and Van Dongen, profoundly disturbed the public and the press by declaring their determination to free painting from its shackles, including naturalistic concerns. They proclaimed that line and colour were to reign supreme, an attitude that sent shock waves through decade after decade of the 20th century. **Thalie Goetz**

SYMBOLISM

During the last quarter of the 19th century, writers and poets reacted against the positivism that marked a world dominated by machines and joined the Symbolist movement, which spread rapidly to the visual arts and included several tendencies (among them, the precursor of the Pre-Raphaelites, founded in 1848). It attracted all sorts of idealists, who had broken with Realism, the official art of the Salons, and Impressionism. The latter privileged sensations, while for the Symbolists, on the contrary, the moving forces behind their art were imagination and dreams. Their favourite subjects were drawn from mythology and the fantastic, and were marked by anguish, silence and death. Several generations were represented; in France, they included Gustave Moreau and Puvis de Chavannes, then Odilon Redon and Paul Gauguin.

Inspired by a poem by Byron about finding Don Juan's body, this canvas illustrates the close relationship that existed between Symbolist literature and painting.
Ford Madox Brown, *The Death of Don Juan*, oil on canvas, 1878.

"The quiet harmony of lines and the vibrant colours penetrate the soul, filling it with heavenly peace and deep, silent joy," wrote Romain Rolland in 1899.
Puvis de Chavannes, *Jeunes Filles au Bord de la Mer*, oil on canvas, 1879.

This pastel, with its daring juxtaposition of colours, is one of the most perfectly finished works of Odilon Redon. It was to incarnate the idea of meditation.
Odilon Redon, *Le Bouddha*, pastel, around 1904-1905.

"... it is the story of her life, her remains. It is the expression of an empassioned soul," was Paul Claudel's reaction to this work by his sister Camille.
Camille Claudel, *L'Age Mûr*, bronze.

ART NOUVEAU

No matter what it was called, be it "Modern Style," "Arte Joven," "Jugenstil" or "Art Nouveau," the new art that developed during the last quarter of the 19th century took on a decidedly international dimension to match its ambitions. Taking up the ideas of such dissidents as Viollet-le-Duc in France or Ruskin in Great Britain, its proponents refused to accept the academic or naturalistic works that had dominated the art scene for several decades. They were in favour of a return to the study nature, with particular emphasis on floral motifs. They were interested in introducing beauty into everyday life and making it accessible to all classes in society. Out of this blossoming of ideas, one can note two main tendencies: one based on floral inspiration, embodied in France by the School of Nancy; the other was a rationalistic trend, represented by the Glasgow School and the Wiener Werkstätte.

Alexandre Charpentier (1856-1909), dining room set, 1900, mahogany, oak and papier wood, gilt-bronze mounts.

François-Rupert Carabin (1862-1932), bookshelf made of walnut wood and wrought iron, 1890. Louis Majorelle (1859-1926), *Orchidées*, a desk made of mahogany, stamped leather and gilt bronze, 1905-1909.

Mackintosh was the moving force behind the Glasgow school. Opposed to the French floral style, he preferred more practical, functional furniture. Charles Rennie Mackintosh (1868-1928), desk made of white lacquered wood, 1904.

An architect and a decorator, Joseph Hoffmann was one of the founders of the Wiener Werkstätte, a company set up to produce art objects for a big buying public. In designing both the house and its interior furnishings, Hoffmann's aim was to create a total art object, a goal artists since Viollet-le-Duc had tried to reach.
Joseph Hoffmann, armchair with adjustable back, bent beech and laminated wood, around 1908.

Thonet Frères, chairs made of bent beech wood and caning, around 1860-1890.

THE RETURN TO CLASSICISM

At the turn of the century, a small number of painters and sculptors stood out because of their common quest for classicism. During his frequent trips to Italy, Maurice Denis found inspiration in the style of the Italian Primitives, in their approach as well as in their colour range and composition. Throughout his diverse decorative styles, he was the proponent of ''a new classical order''. This so-called ''return to style'' was proned in sculpture by Joseph Bernard, Maillol and Bourdelle. They put emphasis on form rather than on subject-matter, taking their inspiration for form from Antiquity. Tired of the technical virtuosity of academic artists and of Rodin's by then somewhat systematic analysis of sentiment, they proned a simplification of form, and were in favour of ''well-balanced, passionless gestures and bodies kept under perfect control'' that expressed a sense of spirituality.

This woman carrying water is a study in rhythm and balance. ''No torsion or parallel limbs that might harm the clarity of the composition, but rather a genuine desire to simplify form.''
Joseph Bernard, *Porteuse d'Eau*, bronze, 1912.

Using a subject from mythology, the sculptor Bourdelle showed complete mastery over his composition. He has a free way of handling his medium that is typical of the 20th century.
Emile-Antoine Bourdelle (1861-1929), *Heraclès Archer*, bronze, 1909.

For Maillol ''art
does not consist in
copying nature.''
He gradually
idealised his model
in the search for a
classical sense of
balance and
harmony.
Aristide Maillol,
Méditerranée, 1905,
marble.

When the Nabi
group broke up,
Maurice Denis
began doing works
with decorative
colours and
rhythms. He put
them to full
advantage, even
in works of
sometimes
monumental
proportions.
Maurice Denis
(1870-1943), *Le Jeu
de Volant*, oil on
canvas, 1900.

In this bas-relief,
Maillol transposed
to sculpture his
experience with
the Nabis. He
developed a style
that in its sobriety
was quite unlike
the Symbolist
outpourings of
many of his fellow
sculptors.
Aristide Maillol
(1861-1944), *Le
Désir*, lead, 1908.

**Painted for the
mother of Robert
Delaunay, this
work was an
updated version of
the "good
savage" done
with a naive
technique and an
unconventional
style.**
Henri Rousseau,
known as Le
Douanier, *La
Charmeuse de
Serpent*, oil on
canvas, 1907.

Henri Julien Rousseau

Though Munch inspired the expressionist painters of Europe, he here leaves off with the Symbolism of the 1890s to paint in a more straight-forward manner. The violent colours herald Fauvism. Edvard Munch, *Summer Night at Aagaarstrand*, oil on canvas, 1904.

PRACTICAL INFORMATION

**Musée d'Orsay
62, rue de Lille
75007 Paris
Main entrance: 1, rue de Bellechasse
Entrance for major exhibitions: Place Henri de Montherlant
General information (answering machine):
45 49 11 11
Group-visit information (answering machine):
45 49 49 49**

OPENING HOURS:

The museum is open to the public on Sunday from 9 am to 6 pm; on Tuesday, Wednesday, Friday and Saturday from 10 am to 6 pm; on Thursday from 10 am to 9.45 pm. Closed on Monday.

FACILITIES:

For the visitor's convenience, the museum offers an information desk, public telephones, mail boxes, a money-exchange bureau, a first-aid station, sales counters for guide books, a bookshop and a postcard stand, a restaurant and a café.

The restaurant is located on the mezzanine level and is open daily at lunchtime and on Thursday evening; closed Monday.

The café on the upper level, known as the "Café des Hauteurs", remains open during museum visiting hours.

Details on various museum activities are available at the reception desk and in "Les Nouvelles du Musée d'Orsay", published every other month.

GUIDED TOURS:

Tours are available daily, except at 11 am on Sunday; additional tour on Thursday at 7 pm. Special tours are also available:
— "A Look at One Work", daily except Sunday, from 12.30 pm to 1.30 pm;
— A department of the museum, daily except Sunday, from 1 pm to 2.30 pm;
— Dossier-exhibitions, from Tuesday to Friday, from 12.30 pm to 1.30 pm. To join the tour, be at the reception desk ("comptoir d'accueil") at 12.15 pm.
— Earphones can be rented at the entrance to the museum.

TEMPORARY EXHIBITIONS:

The museum organizes two types of exhibitions:
— Major exhibitions organized in collaboration with the Réunion des Musées Nationaux (entrance Place de Montherlant);
— Dossier-exhibitions around a theme or a work, which are located at various spots in the museum.

LECTURES, PANEL DISCUSSIONS AND COURSES:

Courses on cultural history are organized by the museum and the Ecole du Louvre on Tuesdays from 6.30 pm to 8 pm. Open to members of the museum, who must sign up in advance.

Lecture series and colloquium are organized in conjunction with major museum activities and are held on Saturdays from 11 am to 12.30 pm. These Saturday lectures are recorded in their entirety and can be listened to in the consulting room above the Café des Hauteurs. The lectures are also published in a volume called "48-14", on sale at the bookshop.

CONCERTS/MUSIC:

Concerts organized at 12.30 pm and at the Salle des Fêtes at 6.30 pm are free for museum visitors. There is a charge for evening concerts held at 8.30 pm in the auditorium. Reservations can be made at the museum or by telephoning 45.49.45.46. Concerts are held in the restaurant on Sundays from 4 pm to 6 pm.

Recordings of these concerts can be bought at the bookshop.

FILMS:

feature-length films and film festivals are shown in the auditorium. The museum also produces documentaries and short films that are shown in the various museum studios.

YOUTH ACTIVITIES:

"Forums for High-School Students": on the first Wednesday of the month, at 3 pm in the auditorium, a high-school class presents one aspect of 19th-century art history. Reserved for high-school students; to register, call 40.49.48.73.

"Open House for Teachers": review of the teaching facilities available at the museum and a

From left to right and from top to bottom: the Passageway of the Press, the auditorium, the area devoted to history, the restaurant, the Café des Hauteurs, the reception room.

visit to an exhibition with the curator in charge. Reserved for teachers. To register, call 40.49.49.49.

Tours (to explore the museum or to visit a workshop) are offered to young people every Wednesday at 2.30 pm. Prior registration required; call 40.49.49.76 or reserve at the reception desk in the "Espace des Jeunes".

DOCUMENTATION:

Information cards are in evidence at various key points in the museum for the visitor's use. In the documentation room located above the Café des Hauteurs, interested visitors will find computerized pictures and documents, as well as books and catalogues.

MEMBERSHIP:

The museum's "Carte Blanche" gives free access to the museum, to lectures and to certain concerts. Members are allowed a 5 per cent reduction on books bought at the museum bookshop and receive by mail the "Nouvelles du Musée d'Orsay". Information available at the museum.

THE BOOKSHOP

The bookshop, designed by Gae Aulenti, is located in what was formerly the buffet of the old railway station. Spread out on two levels, it has a selection of over 10,000 different books, in French as well as in other languages, on the various disciplines in the timespan covered by the museum (1848-1914): painting, architecture, decoration, sculpture, cinema and photography, as well as literature and history.

On the mezzanine, which boasts a frieze done by Mucha for the Exposition Universelle of 1900, visitors can find engravings, casts, reproductions of jewellery made for the most part by the Réunion des Musées Nationaux, as well as fine selection of children's books, games, models and objects. All make original gifts.

On the ground floor are museum guide books, as well as catalogues and publications on special exhibitions devoted to, say, Camille Claudel, Van Gogh in Paris or the Chicago School of Architecture.

Alon with books that trace the history of musical creation from 1848 to 1914, the shop offers a related selection of compact disks.

Major works of French literature are offered in pocket editions, as well as critical works on the movements and fashions of the 19th century, like Dandyism. Travel books of the period, political and sociological studies, and works on daily life in France complete the picture.

Readers will also find a large selection of books on art, including artists' correspondence, biographies and monographs of well known and little known painters and sculptors, and the principal movements in 19th-century art. There are also works on such techniques as lithography, print-making, and pastels. Film-lovers will find a section reflecting that of the museum, with works on the era of silent moving pictures by Melies, Chaplin and Buster Keaton. There are books for photography buffs as well, showing how it became an art form.

A special section is devoted to the great names, schools and movements in architecture and the decorative arts.

Museum visitors can thus find a useful and pleasureable complement to their tour of the museum collections, for the bookshop offers a very complete coverage of literary and artistic creations from 1848 to 1914.

Small offshoots of the bookshop, which offer a selection of guide books, are located at various strategic points in the museum itself. Lastly, a postcard shop gives onto the esplanade in front of the main entrance to the museum; visitors can choose from among 500 reproductions of the paintings, sculpture or objets d'art that they want to remember. **Odile Billoret**

Above and righ-hand page: two views of the bookshop.

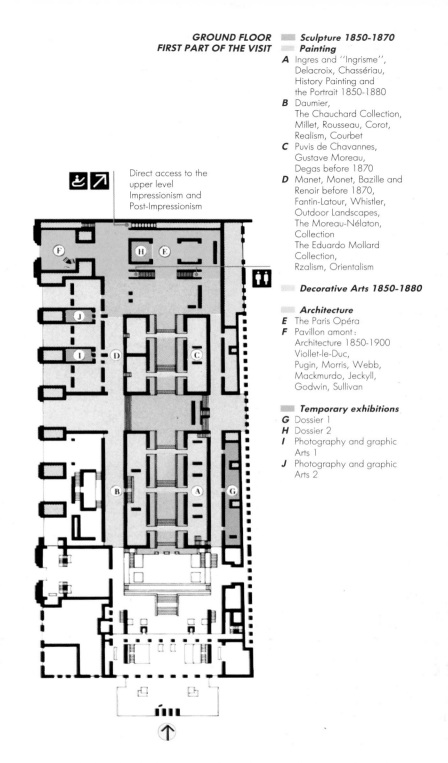

■ *Sculpture 1850-1870*
■ *Painting*

A Ingres and "Ingrisme",
Delacroix, Chassériau,
History Painting and
the Portrait 1850-1880

B Daumier,
The Chauchard Collection,
Millet, Rousseau, Corot,
Realism, Courbet

C Puvis de Chavannes,
Gustave Moreau,
Degas before 1870

D Manet, Monet, Bazille and
Renoir before 1870,
Fantin-Latour, Whistler,
Outdoor Landscapes,
The Moreau-Nélaton,
Collection
The Eduardo Mollard
Collection,
Rzalism, Orientalism

■ *Decorative Arts 1850-1880*

■ *Architecture*

E The Paris Opéra
F Pavillon amont:
Architecture 1850-1900
Viollet-le-Duc,
Pugin, Morris, Webb,
Mackmurdo, Jeckyll,
Godwin, Sullivan

■ *Temporary exhibitions*

G Dossier 1
H Dossier 2
I Photography and graphic
Arts 1
J Photography and graphic
Arts 2

Direct access to the
upper level
Impressionism and
Post-Impressionism

The museum is on three levels, an the permanent collection is shown in more or less chronological order. On the ground floor, the main hall in the centre is devoted to sculpture of the late Neo-Classical and Romantic periods. Beyond it is a room with large models of the Opera house, which itself is flanked by two towers, one of which deals with Grimaud, the other with Art Nouveau. The Opera room gives onto the Architecture Pavilion, where mock-ups and drawings evoke the renaissance of architec-

ture during the 19th century. On either side of the main hall is a succession of rooms devoted to painting. On the right-hand side, the visitor will discover works of the Second Empire, running from Ingres to Degas, that perpetuate tradition as regards both subject-matter and technique. Rooms filled with objets d'art complete the visitor's understanding of this period. On the left-hand side of the main hall are the Realist painters, from Daumier to Millet, Courbet, Manet and Monet, which leads the

visitor quite naturally to Impressionism. The year 1870, when the Franco-Prussian war broke out, marks the end of this first part of the visit.

The second part is situated on the top floor of the museum and consists primarily of paintings, as well as of a few sculptures done by such painters as Degas, Renoir and Gauguin. All the avant-guarde movements in paintings are represented here, from the Impressionists to the Nabis, as are the leading artists in each movement: